I0170296

MORE
AND MORE
EACH DAY

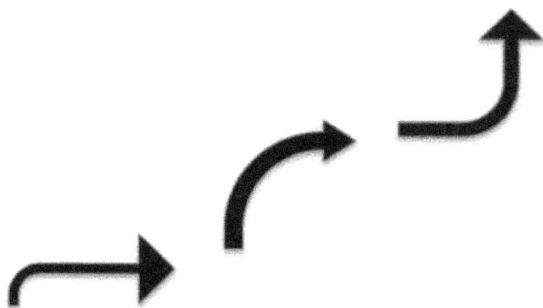

*A Poetic Praise For
Healing and Prospering
The Mind, Body and Spirit*

By: Paul T. Winfield, PhD

©2017 Deva*Ink* Publishing
www.devaink.com

Dedication:

*For those that bless others
And for those in opportunity to receive*

*For those that have taught me love by their
example
And for those that showed me the results of fear*

*For Rita and WT, Darlene and Bill, Tim, Nia,
Rachel, Victoria, Ace, Liam & Muh*

*For Angie, Antoine, Britni, Filip, Kevin, Jamye,
John, Mona, Vanessa & Howard*

*For my guides:
Lady Lee Andrews, James Baldwin,
Michael Bernard Beckwith,
Harry Belafonte, Eric Butterworth,
Pedro Albizu Campos, Paulo Coehlo,
Angela Davis, Dr. Wayne Dyer,
Charles and Myrtle Filmore, Paulo Friere,
Marcus Garvey, Paul Hasselbeck,
Langton Hughes, Dr. Huey P. Newton,
Bayard Rustin, Don Miguel Ruiz,
Sidney Portier, Rev. Sylvia Sumter,
Bishop Desmond Tutu,
Neale Diamond Walsh,
The Foundation for Inner Peace and
Unity Worldwide Ministries*

I love you!! Thank You!!

CONTENTS

Introduction

Although I have been on a spiritual journey throughout my entire life, the last four years have been especially affirmational of who I am and what I believe. I grew up in a Black Baptist Church with all the love you would hope for but with all the trappings of traditional thought too. I don't believe everything that I did back then and certainly not in the same way. Back then I believed innocently, as my parents, grandparents and elders told me what was true. Now I have some evidence based on my experience to add to that wisdom which makes my truths more real in my life.

Five years ago, I was laid off from a job that I loved that also lacked growth potential. To be honest, the business was downsizing, actually dying, a far cry from opening a path for my growth. That challenge was one of the greatest blessing in my life, as it opened the door for me to make a change and follow my heart. I had always dreamed of being a Doctor (PhD, not medical). I had wanted to be Dr. Winfield for as long as I can remember.

I think I considered it "normal" because I was educated in a program that required all of my teachers from the 1ˢᵗ grade on to have a PhD. I always wanted it, I always desired it, I always believed it was for me. So it was no surprise when I started a PhD program in 2004. But life happened and I got distracted. My belief was not certain knowledge of the inevitability of achievement, but rather a certainty in my capacity. I knew I could do it, in a hypothetical sense, but I was not taking steps to actively achieve this lifelong goal.

Then suddenly, I didn't have an excuse. The economy was still challenging for finding new employment, but I was laid off, so I had a bit of a severance package. I also had generous supportive parents, a loving family & friendship network, a great academic program that worked with me, and of course the capacity to achieve. All I had to do, was do it. Take one step in front of the other, towards my goal: PhD. Two years later, I had my degree in hand, no longer a hypothetical dream, but an actual reality.

This time also introduced me to Unity Worldwide ministries, cementing my knowledge of New Thought theology. After I graduated, and still did not find a job, I moved to Puerto Rico, which allowed me to fully slow down and make time and space for me. After five transformational years of reading, breathing, thinking, integrating knowledge with life, practicing yoga, meditating, praying, singing, shouting, crying, some things have become crystal clear for me. The first is that we all, as humans have unlimited power. We can have whatever we want. We can do whatever we want. We can be whatever we want. We just have to want it, and put forth energy in that direction.

One of the tools that has helped me achieve efficiently, effectively and quickly is developing a personal spiritual practice. My spiritual practice grew from that Black Baptist Christian church experience of my formative years. Therefore, terms like blessings and prayers and God resonate with me. If those terms don't work for you, change them. Use Source. Use energy. Whatever is in alignment for you, is what you should use. You will know because it is comforting to you, not in any way stress inducing.

My practice started with prayer as that was the language that was home to me. I then incorporated yoga and meditation. I next integrated mantras to help focus my mind and my energy. Now my spiritual practice also includes my diet and what I feed myself to power this dynamic system I consciously operate.

This book is meant to be an inspirational and motivational collection of poetry and praise to help you tap into your own truth and live your most joyful life. This three-part work offers powerful mantras to help the healing of your mind, a unique prayer which may open you up to the restoration of the body and blessings for the prospering of spirit. These messages should be read daily and serve as a wonderful compliment to meditation, yoga, or whatever spiritual practice you have.

The mantras all come from my practice and powerful messages I have learned along the journey. Although these concepts are typical of New Thought, I have not yet seen them together in a book like this. I offer this book to the world not as a how to "Guide" book, because I cannot tell you how to get closer to yourself. That is a journey only you can take and thus only you can be the expert of. What I can do is offer some provocative thoughts to help guide you on your journey to self-discovery, exploration and realization.

In reading the text, you may notice that AM is always capitalized when following I. That is to remind you that "I Am" is your POWER. Whatever you say you are, is indeed the truth. So, if you say you are sick, then so be it, you are sick. If you say you are wealthy, then that is your truth, even if the appearance in your experience does not yet align with the reality you envision. Just keep practicing, keep speaking it into existence. Eventually what you see in the exterior world will be what you have declared.

As you go on this journey, you will find many of these pages are largely blank. That is intentional. You should only work on one mantra at a time. That may be one per day, or one per meditation session, or one per week. You determine the pace of your experience. But each mantra should be focused on for the time that you focus on it. Then notice if that thought affects you in anyway, or if you have ideas that grow from that thought. If so, feel free to write them down in the space provided. The same is true of the prayers and the blessings.

The prayer section is actually one prayer, based on "The Our Father" or "The Lord's Prayer." After you go through it piece by piece, I encourage you to read it as one prayer, and if so inclined write your own version of the prayer that resonates with you.

Finally, the blessing section is a powerful way to raise the energy level of your environment and the world. By blessing others, you send those you care about (and even those that you don't) love and light. The more good energy we focus into our world, the better experience we will have.

This is your life. You can make of it whatever you want. You are unlimited. It is my intention that this book help you tap into your true power. You are a Diva/Deva and by definition you are a powerful creator of your experience of life. If you want, make it great, make it pretty, make it joyful, make it prosperous!! Why? Because you can, so why not?

Blessings on the Journey and Much Love,

Dr. Paul

MANTRAS for the Mind

A mantra is a thought that you repeat silently or aloud to help you focus on an idea. Use one mantra per meditation session, day or week as you like. If you receive any messages or have any new thoughts feel free to write them down in the space provided or in the notebook of your choice.
Nameste!!

More and more each day,
I Am love.

I Am healthier,
more and more each day.

More and more each day
I Am creative.

I Am more and more wealthy
each day.

More and more each day,
I Am secure.

I Am worthy more and more
each day.

More and more each day
I Am light.

I Am knowing more and more each day.

More and more each day
I Am joy.

I Am blessing more and more
each day.

More and more each day
I Am grateful.

I Am more and more beautiful
each & every day.

More and more each day
I Am confident.

I Am more and more peaceful
each day.

More and more each day
I Am visionary.

I Am wiser
more and more each day.

More and more each day
I Am vocal.

I Am more and more generous
each day.

*More and more each day
I Am powerful.*

*I Am perfecting more and more
each day.*

More and more each day
I Am overflowing.

I Am more and more clairvoyant
each day.

*More and more each day
I Am listening.*

*I Am more and more declarative
each day.*

More and more each day
I Am resurrection.

I Am growing
more and more each day.

More and more each day
I Am life.

I Am more and more
the way each day.

More and more each day
I Am truth.

I Am more and more prosperous each day.

More and more each day
I Am happy.

I Am more and more regeneration
each day.

More and more each day
I Am radiant.

I forgive myself
more and more each day.

More and more each day
I Am rich.

I Am growing younger more and more each day.

More and more each day
I Am amazing.

More and more each day love, success, health and
prosperity are finding their way into my life.

*More and more each day, I forgive others for
everything in the past.*

*I gratefully enjoy and happily share my blessings
more and more each day.*

More and more each day I keep my thoughts
focused on what I desire manifest.

More and more each day I see the world as myself.

*More and more each day I Am radiating love,
peace, light, health and joy.*

*More and more each day I give thanks for my
many blessings.*

I Am healthier, more and more each day.

More and more each day, I Am fun.

PRAYER FOR THE BODY

A prayer is a communication from your conscious mind to your unconscious mind. Some call this unconscious part of yourself, God, or universal energy. This communication helps you release the stress of the conscious world providing the space for health to flow in. As with the mantras, move through these thoughts at your own pace, trying to think as deeply as possible on each idea. If you receive any messages or have any new thoughts feel free to write them down in the space provided or in the notebook of your choice.
Nameste!!

MOTHER
FATHER
HOLY SOURCE

I Am conscious of
the Infinite Power
in whom I live and
by which I create.

LOVE, LIGHT, UNITY,
HEALTH, WHOLENESS,
INTELLIGENCE AND PROSPERITY
ARE OUR EVER-EXPANDING NATURE.

**Unlimited perfection
in idea and manifestation,
I Am Divine Expression
with Intention.**

IN GRATITUDE I RECEIVE

MY DAILY SUPPLY OF
ABUNDANT SUBSTANCE

AS I CELEBRATE THE CONTINUOUS DEMONSTRATION OF JOYFUL LIFE WITH PURPOSE.

**THE LOVING SPIRIT
REMOVES FROM MY AWARENESS,
ANY ILLUSIONS OF CONDEMNATION
OF MYSELF OR OTHERS.**

As forgiveness effectively
helps us
Practice and Remember
our Oneness,

I FORGIVE EVERYONE FOR EVERYTHING.

**WITH APPRECIATION,
MORE AND MORE EACH DAY
I AM LOVING, JOYFUL, PEACEFUL,
PATIENT, KIND, GOOD, FAITHFUL,
GENTLE, AND WISELY FOCUSED.**

Thanks God: My Director of Ambition,

My Avenue to Achievement,

AND THE GLORY OF SUCCESS

**FOR ALL THAT I AM
TO BE, DO AND HAVE.**

ALL IS WELL AND ON TIME, AT ALL TIMES.

THIS IS THE TRUTH!!

IT IS NOW DONE!!
AND SO IT IS!!

Paul's Prayer

Mother Father Holy Source,
I Am conscious of the Infinite Power
in whom I live and by which I create.

Love, Light, Unity, Health,
Wholeness, Intelligence and Prosperity
are Our ever-expanding nature.
Unlimited Perfection in Idea and Manifestation,
I Am Divine Expression with Intention.

In gratitude I receive
my daily supply of abundant substance
as I celebrate the continuous demonstration
of joyful life with purpose.

The Loving Spirit removes from my awareness,
any illusions of condemnation of myself or others.
As forgiveness effectively helps us
Practice and Remember our Oneness,
I forgive Everyone for Everything.

With appreciation, more and more each day
I Am loving, joyful, peaceful, patient, kind,
good, faithful, gentle, and wisely focused.

Thanks God: My Director of Ambition,
My Avenue to Achievement, and the Glory of
Success
for all that I Am to Be, Do and Have.

All is well and on time, at all times.
This is the Truth!!
It is now Done!! And so it is!

<u>Your Prayer</u>

BLESSINGS FOR THE SPIRIT

A blessing is sending positive energy in a focused, concentrated way to the target of your direction. The added bonus is that blessing others is also the fastest way to receive a blessing. These blessings here may be used for yourself or others. You may want to use one blessing per day or you may prefer to be more generous. Whatever you like, you cannot be to generous with blessings as there is always more. If you receive any messages or have any new thoughts feel free to write them down in the space provided or in the notebook of your choice.
Nameste!!

*More and more each day
I bless who I am and how I feel.*

*More and more each day
I bless my family and send them love, light, peace,
joy and prosperity.*

I bless my body which is growing more and more strong, gorgeous & healthy each day.

.

More and more each day
I bless my friends and send them love, light, peace, health, joy and prosperity.

More and more each day
I bless my growing abundance.

More and more each day
I bless my home and how I live.

More and more each day
I bless my inflow of resources and community.

I bless my mind more and more each day
and celebrate the many wonderful ideas it creates.

I love myself more and more each day.

I accept myself more and more each day.

More and more each day
I realize anything is possible.

More and more each day
I appreciate miracles are happening in my life.

*I realize I am in the flow of life
more and more each day.*

*I Am filled with love peace and joy more and more
each day.*

More and more each day
I Am free of pain, illness and disease.

More and more each day
I am blessed with amazing great fortune.

*More and more each day limiting thoughts of
diagnosis are burning in the light of truth that
I Am whole, clean and increasingly healthy.*

*More and more each day
I bless others to be, do and have as they want.*

More and more each day
I give myself permission to be, do and have
whatever I want.

More and more each day
I give others permission to be, do and have
whatever they want.

Conclusion

Well, I hope you enjoyed sharing this part of the journey. I encourage you to continue developing your practice. Continue living your life as joyfully as possible. Remember that you can do whatever you want. First get a clear idea about what you want, no matter how "big" it looks. The more you reach for the stars, the greater the likelihood of you actually getting off the ground.

Believe you can do it. Believe God, the Universe, energy or whatever brings you comfort is working to help you. Consider your dream to be a premonition of what's your possible future if you keep believing. Use the mantra's and prayers to help encourage yourself and remind yourself of your unlimited power. Then do everything you can to bless yourself and others; especially others. The more you give, the more you receive, so bless, bless, bless!!

I send you peace, love, health, joy and prosperity. Its really that simple. I bless you, and so it is. Be blessed!! Nameste.

ABOUT THE AUTHOR

Dr. Paul is a strategist, scholar, entrepreneur, world explorer, truth student and change agent. He has worked, studied or lived on six continents in 10 nations, and traveled through over 60 countries. A portfolio manager with 15 years experience, Paul has served a variety of agencies to promote individual and cooperative development. Paul lives excellence by encouraging the very best in others. With a gentle spirit, sharp mind, & passion for helping those in need, Paul combines the benefits of strategic planning and critical thinking to overcome systemic challenges.

When Dr. Paul is not writing or researching, he works with clients to develop business and community through strategic planning, data analysis, financial & project management. He has represented Associations at national conferences, and collaborated with other advocates to develop policy recommendations directed at improving the quality of life for underserved populations in terms of justice, health and community relations.

In achieving his doctorate, Paul successfully completed a rigorous academic program demanding knowledge and utilization of statistical analysis, comprehensive program monitoring and evaluation, experience internationally in South America and Africa, and a dissertation analyzing the first, comprehensive domestic United States HIV/AIDS policy with an intersectional focus on Black gay men.

Previously, Paul managed a variety of projects for both non-profit and for-profit organizations, consulting domestically. Serving in Academic

Affairs, he was the primary liaison between students and administration, frequently facilitating conflict resolution on behalf of students. As Financial Management Consultant, he effectively promoted the development of an inner-city community literacy program. He advised the Board of Directors on financial and organization matters, and also managed successful large development events, In working with a small for-profit business, Dr. Paul achieved disadvantaged business status certifications and developed marketing strategies to improve their capacity for acquiring contracts, leading to sustained growth.

Dr. Paul also successfully completed major projects for three organizations internationally. In Morocco, he developed and managed the planning and execution of a one-week conference with participants from 15 countries. In Kenya, Dr. Paul managed all student affairs responsibilities for a research institute. This included the planning and execution of all excursions, which investigated HIV/AIDS throughout Kenya. He also managed student conflicts and health challenges as presented. In Uruguay, he developed a five-year strategic plan for a non-profit partner with the United Nations Children's Fund (UNICEF).

Currently, Paul is contributing to the restoration of his home town of Baton Rouge, Louisiana after the destructive Great Floods of 2016 and his chosen home of San Juan, Puerto Rico in their recovery from the hurricanes Irma and Maria of 2017.

www.ingramcontent.com/pod-product-compliance
Lightning Source LLC
Chambersburg PA
CBHW031607040426
42452CB00006B/438